TABLE OF CONTENTS

Prologue

Thank you for expressing your interest to read about my life journey. I had originally written about My Life Journey on a blogging platform. This sequence was read by some of my friends who found it inspiring. I have attempted to share some of my personal experiences of my professional career path in a simplistic manner.

Youngsters fresh out of college and looking to start a professional career can refer to this book as a learning of some of the do's and don'ts during your career path. I have simply shared my experiences and my approach – simply focus on completing the action items in my hands. My work spoke for me which echoed louder than my voice and words.

Experienced people can refer to my book for getting tips on how to grow professionally in their career. Movements and promotions need not be horizontal, rather they are most effective when they are diagonal. Diagonal promotions mean a combination of lateral and vertical movements, which may happen simultaneously or separately. This makes for a better growth and widening of roles and responsibilities resulting in a holistic approach.

Disclaimer

Dedications

This book is dedicated to my loving mother and my beloved wife who have always stood by me, through thick and thin, through adversity and prosperity, happiness and sadness, through quarrels and re-unions, etc.

Credits to my schoolteachers and school mates who have grown with me with teaching, learning, funning, punning, fighting, uniting, playing, competing, etc.

Credits to all the people around me who have stood by me through thick and thin, physically or mentally, personally or virtually, on or off social media, tenured or youngsters, etc.

Last but not the least, credits to the reader and writer, hunter and hunted, agents and supervisors, team leaders and managers, colleagues, peers and teammates, friends and acquaintances, online and offline, etc., to provide such inspiring stories and incidents for me to pen them into a book. You may or may not have served me directly or indirectly, but now it's payback time from you to me via me authoring and monetizing this book. 😊

Note from the Author

Dear Reader,

My gratitude to you for taking the time to read this book. You are concerned about your career and future. I have simply re-lived my life beginning from the end of my college days. I have narrated the different stages of my professional journey in various chapters, the way any young college graduate would live his/her life.

I have laid down my experiences in the form of simple to read and understand words. The intent of this book is to share the learnings from experience during my entire professional career.

I trust this book will give you some good insights which can possibly help improve your professional journey one step at a time. Wish you all the very best in your endeavor to bring about this change in attitude and perspective towards your career.

Yours truly,

Ayaz Shabbir Zanzeria

Chapter 1 – The Beginning

Introduction

Born in an orthodox family, I was rebellious since my childhood days and had a habit of questioning conventional approaches and methods. For this reason, I would never get along with any of my immediate and extended family members. However, this taught me to live independently and make my own decisions—irrespective of size and type.

School Life

During school, I loved playing table tennis, carrom and chess. These were my favorites and I used to feature in the top 5 in regular (unofficial) tournaments with my fellow students. As part of self-defense techniques, I learnt a bit of martial arts and boxing.

School life was full of fun, frolic, learning, madness, fighting, arguments, debates, discussions, playfulness, growth, personal socializing, etc. These were the best years of my life. The relations formed are memorable even today. Whenever I meet my school friends, most of our conversations begin with "Do you remember..." This is a different feeling altogether.

College Life

Junior college had its own set of learnings and adventures. College days was as good as living a movie in real life, especially with some of the more adventurous "Romeos" or "passionate lovers". These were the type who would go to any extent for their girls. Including shedding blood—either their own or someone else's.

Senior college had its own share of learnings and adventures in store for me. This was the beginning of another phase of an independent journey. Four years of engineering had its own set of ups and downs. This was the time when I learnt socializing and networking the old-fashioned and practical way—meet people face to face, talk to them, exchange conversations and keep in touch via regular phone calls. Those were the good old days without internet, without social media (no Facebook, no LinkedIn, no twitter, no Instagram, no smartphones, no gadgets).

Technology Status

This was an era where pagers were considered a luxury. First, it was numeric pagers followed by alpha-numeric pagers. To send a message, we needed to call the contact center and either tell the number or message or both. Then came the mobile phone with the good old "snake" game. This was such a huge hit on the monochrome screen that it literally made people addicted to it! Drugs and alcohol were not that addictive at that time! People would buy expensive mobile phones only for the snake game.

Monochrome brick sized phones slowly shrunk and evolved into smarter colorful phones with cameras. Clicking pictures with a mobile was considered a luxury. Then evolved the touch screen phones and today, we know the current scenario of mobile phones especially smartphones.

Engineering College Life

Coming back to my learning engineering days in college, this was an adventure of sorts in which I met a few of my old adversaries. I got the experience of meeting a "girlfriend" who gave me an "illusion" of love. These four years were filled with its own set of adventure, learning, networking, socializing, meeting new people, building contacts, participating in events, organizing events, etc. My personal favorite event was the blood donation camp that we used to organize in our college. In my days, we used to have record collections (as per our college standards).

In my final year of engineering, I was the envy of my classmates due to the reach of my social network and my ability to do the projects of my classmates (for a fee). I had personally completed my project late for various other reasons, however, I ensured that I helped all my other classmates to complete their projects on time. Of course, I charged them a small fee for this and earned quite a decent amount of money. Hence, this was one of my early ventures or stages of independent earnings.

Synopsis

This was the first chapter in which I have described the initial days of my life consisting of my academic and educational career upto my graduation. This was the preparation stage for the longer duration of my professional career. My focus was to complete my studies at the earliest to get a good job with a decent salary.

Chapter II – Baby Steps

Introduction

The first chapter of my life journey outlines my childhood and youth days in school and college. I also mentioned about the lifestyle back then in the absence of technology, internet, social media, emails, etc. In this, we will look at some of the events that occurred in the early days of my professional career.

After college, I got a job in an automobile company. Although the learning was good, it was restricted. As an inexperienced novice, I took the job very lightly and quit within six months. During my tenure in this company, the only factor that I enjoyed was the feel of driving a car on a very small, limited part of Mumbai roads.

Job in IT Sector

After quitting this job, I started my job hunt by reading newspapers and manually sending out paper applications to different companies and offices. I went down to a few of these places and spoke to people. Job hunting at that time had a different flavor altogether especially with the paper applications, personal meetings with the HR and hiring managers. This was the absence of technology of the good old days. Chances of your resume being picked up and seen was much higher. People would spend much more time reading and understanding your resume in its entirety and then asking questions in an interview.

My next target was a job in which I could learn computers and earn. I did not want to spend money on learning computer courses. I did manage to get my "desired" job in a reputed computer institute as a lecturer. I was given training on the job to fulfil my role. This was the time when I learnt Java programming language with its related technologies—SQL, Java Servlets, Enterprise Java Beans, etc. I was ecstatic. I did not limit my knowledge and learning to the courseware and explored further. My fame and popularity grew in leaps and bounds.

Rise to Fame

This was the time in which some of the students would ask for me and take admission to learn courses. Some of them completed Level 1 and Level 2 certifications successfully in the very first attempt under my guidance. Most of them got good high-paying jobs at that time—these were some of my major unsung achievements although my salary was just a fraction of what they got. However, monetary rewards were not my goal.

I was among the elite few Java lecturers who were selected to travel to different parts of the country sponsored by the company to train others. My working etiquettes and style of communication had earned me a reputation that people would look forward to learning from me. I had the record of gaining the maximum attendance consistently. This became the source of envy for some of my other colleagues. Some even went to the extent of playing dirty games (corporate politics) with me, however, that was not a deterrent for me from completing my tasks.

It was during this time, that I even managed to witness a couple of horrific scenes. One was the love story of a boy and a girl in which the boy took a dangerous and risky step of stabbing the girl. The girl happened to be the daughter of a police inspector. The other scene that I witnessed was the cheapness at which a young ambitious girl would stoop to move up the corporate ladder. These were simply glimpses of what I was to face next.

The IT recession of 2001 was one of the hard-hitting ones and this institute was severely impacted. Hence, I had to quit out of my own free will (although I was never asked to quit; however, I was not retained either) and look for a new job. Then started a fresh round of job hunting in which I managed to land a job in another vehicle service center. Although I was here for a few months, I was not happy and was looking to move out.

Chapter III – First Venture into Entrepreneurship

Introduction

This is a continuation of my life journey. In the previous chapters, I had described the initial stage of my professional career. At the point of taking a break of the story, there was a short transition in my professional career life from a working person to an entrepreneur. Yes, this was way back in the year 2001 when I thought of starting my own Internet Cafe.

First venture into entrepreneurship

I did manage to do the initial setup especially for the hardware and the software. However, the downside was that I did not get my internet connection on time thanks to the lethargic government agencies. That was not a deterrent for me as I had listed a variety of services including a gaming center for kids. That went well in which kids used to pay a small amount of money every hour to play games.

I used to offer training courses as an additional service. The idea was good, however, the people in the locality who would visit me, either wanted the services for free or were reluctant to pay my requested fee. Sadly, they would even fight to shell out money despite being informed of the rates well in advance. That will still not a deterrent for me as I started to build my online presence slowly and steadily.

Failure of my first venture

I had to shut down my business within a couple of months due to lack of opportunities and funding at that time. However, that small stint was a wonderful learning experience. Other people from the same area gave me friendly advice and tips on how to start a business. Remember, way back in the early 2000s, to start and run your own business was a different ball game altogether. Yes, I was approached by another company who had a network of internet cafes pan India to join their network. I refused due to lack of initial capital for further investment.

After downing the shutter, I had five computers, a printer and a scanner at my disposal. I sold four in a bid to recover some of the initial capital that I had invested. Yes, I managed to successfully do that. The printer and scanner at that time were the best of their class, hence, I had retained them for some time. I spent at least a month in clearing off all debts by selling off or liquidating the remainder of my assets. This was an experience of sorts for me as I wanted to ensure that I would sleep in peace without any debtors knocking at my door.

Synopsis

This was an era in which it was difficult to get a loan without any kind of stable income. Although I have taken several loans for almost ten years, for business, I never really felt the "urge" to take a loan of any sort—from a bank, from an investor or any other source. My dad would always tell me, "Do business on your own merit". This was a statement that has been with me throughout my entire life.

This was a short description of my stint as an entrepreneur. This experience was like "tiger tasting blood and wanting more". When did the next round happen? What did I do next? More to come in the subsequent chapters. Keep reading this book for subsequent parts of my life journey.

Chapter IV – Job Hunting

Introduction

If you have reached this far, it implies that you have read the first three chapters of my life journey and are curious to know what was in store for me after I downed the shutters on my first venture in entrepreneurship. Read on to know what happened next.

Current Job Market Scenario

The year was 2002 and the "call center" type companies had begun a hiring spree. I decided to give it a shot and went for an interview. I realized that the salaries offered were much higher compared to the regular companies. Hence, there was a huge rush of people from all over to try their luck. At that time, I decided to join the bandwagon and started reaching out to companies either directly and/or via other placement consultants.

Travelling was tiring, time-consuming and pocket burning for me. To save some expenses, I used to prefer the cheapest modes of transport—walking, local trains, buses, or other forms of shared transport. To help me cope up with the heat of the sun, I had to consume plenty of liquids. The first, best and cheapest option was sweet lime juice.

Job hunting as an adventure of sorts

Job hunting was not an easy task considering the travel involved. I had to reach places that were either very distant or not easily accessible. Some of the offices had to be reached via multiple modes of transport. I did it in all weathers. Be it sunshine or rain, I did reach different places on time. I used to sit in the lounges and waiting rooms with the other jobseekers. We would strike conversations on their experiences, other job openings, and exchanged contact info.

There were occasions in which I would reach the interview office fully drenched in rain and then sit for hours in the air conditioned cold. Shivering and trying to keep warm, I patiently awaited my turn with the others. Sometimes, the security guards would have pity, but they too were helpless. This hardship had to be borne and endured and came free as a package deal with the job hunt. Effectively, I had to ensure that I was pushing the tolerance levels of my body and not giving in to the torturous conditions that my body was subject to.

During these job hunting days, I had to personally go to meet the recruiters and hiring managers, give them a printed copy of my resume, have an initial conversation with them, exchange contact numbers and get an immediate response from them whether I had been selected for the next round or not. In some cases, I attended multiple interview rounds before getting a final answer. The encouraging factor was that I did get a definite answer, even if it was a no., I did not have to do multiple follow ups for a response.

Synopsis

After being rejected in more than 20 companies and by several placement consultants, after hunting for a tiring three months, I finally landed a job in a contact center. Incidentally, at the same time, I also got an offer to teach Java in a college to aspiring college students. After careful evaluation of my options, I took up both offers and had income coming in from two sources.

This was the job-hunting phase of my life journey. This marked the beginning of my comprehensive professional career, which will be described in the subsequent chapters.

Introduction

In the previous chapter, I described my job-hunting journey way back in the early 2000s. Internet usage, emails, social media were in their infancy. Applications sent online were looked at very rarely. Job hunting in those days meant to scan physical newspapers, write down various addresses, carry multiple copies of your resume with your other documents (for spot offers), travel to those places, meet the recruiters and hiring managers personally, hand over your resume to them and have a conversation with them after hours of waiting with the other candidates.

Life in a Contact Center

My first job in a "call center" or a BPO (Business Process Outsourcing) center was more of an enjoyment rather than a serious job. I was employed for nearly six months in which we used to play, laugh, joke, flirt, watch movies, eat, drink (not liquor) and sleep during our shifts. We would get our salaries very late. To sustain, I took up another job in parallel as a lecturer in a college. This way, I managed to survive on multiple jobs. I did this for nearly three long tiring months.

Teaching college students was a different ball game altogether. They were young, bright, smart, intelligent and very respectful. They were eager to learn especially from teachers who they liked and chose to learn from. I was one of the lucky ones. After their academic year ended, my contract ended too. However, I was called again to teach for another year. This was based on the feedback provided by the students who had learnt from me.

Job change

After my initial hiccup of working in my first call center, I got a job in another reputed company where I spent nearly eight months. Then, I moved on to another company with an anticipation of a salary hike. I did get the salary hike and stayed there for nearly eighteen months. However, I was not happy with the working conditions. The management treated us like "humanoid answering machines". We were not allowed to have human emotions, we were not allowed to fall ill, we were not allowed to live our personal life. All of these under the pretext of "our company is certified, and we need to maintain a high level of compliance". I felt suffocated and moved on.

Synopsis

For getting a job at an "entry level associate" in a call center was comparatively easy – especially if you are not looking for a specific designation or a job profile. All you need is to have good English language communication skills. I had that in me thanks to the solid foundation laid during my school days. This had immensely helped me secure all my "call center" or "contact center" jobs. Later, I realized that they were more correctly known as "BPOs".

Then, I entered a telecom company where I spent nearly five years of my professional career. This was an interesting uphill and upward journey full of learning, adventure, promotions, relations, risks, rewards, transfers, upward and lateral movements, et al. I shall describe this journey in detail in the next chapters.

Chapter VI – Stint in Telecom

Introduction

After reading the first five chapters of this series, you would have known about the good old days and the initial struggle that I had faced during my journey through various phases. My father had passed away before I took admission in an Engineering college for a degree course. The initial grief was too great as it was a tender age for me. However, I managed to get over it and moved on with life without resorting to any vices (fortunately).

Telecom job experience

Continuing from chapter five, my professional journey in the telecom company was the beginning of an uphill and upward undertaking for me in many ways. During my initial days of joining the company, I had to answer phone calls and respond to customer queries and resolve customer complaints. Initially, it was fun, however, I realized that it was easier said than done. The job was becoming more and more monotonous for me and I was thinking of ways of how I could stand out from the crowd.

During my tenure, I never stuck to the only task of taking calls. Rather, I used to experiment and research using the available resources at hand. Although there were systems in place to measure quantitative data, I wanted to verify the information without asking for access. I took an unconventional approach of gathering my own data from the available resources. Hence, I created my own trackers and maintained them.

Gaining visibility

These helped me to validate the appraisal data which I then challenged. My managers were taken aback as they had never faced this before in this manner. Previous challenges from other employees were without data and I was an exception to this. Hence, for them, this was a situation that had to be dealt with in a different way. The data manager met me personally for this and realized that my data was more accurate (a truly exception scenario that I had managed to create with my approach).

Lateral movements and dynamic job roles

My skills and abilities stood by me to ensure my selection for various upcoming projects which needed constant research even with the limited resources at hand. I was selected for various roles and positions in different teams, customer service, first line technical support, second line technical support, mobile number portability, upgrades, retentions, change management, quality team reports, operations analyst, etc. With all of these roles, I was assigned differing responsibilities with an ever-changing job description.

Hence, I had a multitude of roles, responsibilities, tasks and activities to fulfil during my stint of nearly five years. I managed to earn the title of "Solution Provider" irrespective of my designation, department, team or role. This was an achievement for me, although I did not realize it, nor did I pay much heed to it. All I knew was that people at all levels were looking up to me for several positive reasons.

First major impactful project

Before quitting, I had undertaken a project to develop an automated reporting dashboard in MS Excel. I did this while learning macros. This was a huge hit for all the employees at all levels. This was a project that nobody had dared to undertake for fear of failure and criticism. However, I took the bold step forward and succeeded with flying colors. Sadly, corporate politics got to me and thanks to my sycophant manager, I had to quit the company and move on.

The next company that I had joined was a mortgage company which had its own set of adventures and learning. This adventure will be described in the next chapters.

Chapter VII – Mortgage Industry

Introduction

Thank you for reading so far about my life journey. The previous chapter described my adventure in a telecom company where I invested a little under five years of my life. It was in this company that I learnt about the intricacies about branding, difference between branding and marketing, internal communications, corporate politics, et al. Some of the managers that I had worked with, did appreciate my efforts and the changes that I had brought about with the outcomes. However, I had to move on.

Entry into finance – mortgage processing

My next company was a mortgage default processing company which had recently started operations. I was lucky to join at a time when they were celebrating their first anniversary of operations. The technology setup was in its infancy and I was a part of this setup for the operations team. In fact, I was roped in for this purpose. I put my head down to make a list of all the manual tasks and then went about my duties to automate them using MS Office products. Within three months, I managed to free up time and resources with my efforts with simple basic automation using VBA macros.

Beginning of automation and project management

For a growing company, I started my involvement in larger projects, although my participation was at a much smaller level. However, my contribution was significant. Within nine months of joining, I got my first promotion in terms of designation and salary. Subsequent promotions were in terms of roles and responsibilities but not in designation. I was fine with that as I had partially lost interest in the system of promotions. I had settled in my comfort zone in my set of current roles and responsibilities. There were plenty of learnings involved during my tenure.

There were days when I had spent days and nights continuously in office. My boss was very supportive, and he would ensure my wellbeing during these days. Between the two of us, we developed a reputation of "getting work done no matter what". We were considered the "creative and resilient support team" during our days and we laid the foundation of our team. Our team then expanded with diversified roles and responsibilities.

Project and process automation

As the workload grew, we embarked on an automation spree with macros in every product of the MS Office suite (Outlook, Word, Excel, PowerPoint, Access). We commissioned a dedicated system to house the automated reports, internal database, important documents, etc. This was an ecosystem that we setup with documented procedures for audit, compliance and governance. We were considered the governing authority for reports, dashboards and automation in our department (operations support).

Evolution

We then evolved into an admin support team as well. We supported the operations team across geographies. We handled some of the financial processes also. Hence, we had diversified responsibilities and I had thrived in this team by accumulating a wealth of learning that involved technical, administration, audit, compliance, governance, team handling, client relations, and much more. I invested a little under five years of my career journey in this company to amass the experience and learning.

Chapter VIII – Déjà vu with Telecom

Introduction

Thank you for reading and following the first seven chapters of my life journey. If you are here, it simply implies that you have been intrigued by my journey so far and would like to know more about me. I will not disappoint you. At this point, let's take a quick recap into chapter six and cover some aspects of this part of the journey.

Reputation and fame

In chapter six, I mentioned that I had a job in a telecom company and that I had moved from one department to another thus fulfilling various job roles. Each role had its own set of responsibilities, skills and learnings. I displayed the ability to fulfil each of them with utmost finesse. This was seen by the managers and other peers and thus earned me the reputation of a "solution provider", irrespective of my designation and department. Without my knowledge, I was discussed as "problem? go to Ayaz and you will definitely get a solution!" Honestly, this was a surprise and a compliment for me!

Maiden automation project – DR SPOC

This is the time where I undertook an automation project using MS Office products (XL, Word, Access, Outlook, VBA) without much prior knowledge of these products!! However, I put my head down and spent some time in researching the internet on how I can use a combination of these with macros and VBA. By God's Grace, my efforts and perseverance paid off and I was able to develop a front-end tool to auto-generate majority of the reports needed by the operations and other support teams.

This was a huge achievement for me, and I was nicknamed after my tool as "<u>DR SPOC</u>". "DR SPOC" was an acronym for Direct Reporting Single Point of Contact. I loved it and enjoyed every moment of it. This was my first and major automation project which I had undertaken. I launched and maintained it single-handedly for nearly one year until i quit the company. At that time, although I was not sure about linking MS XL with MS Access, I found ways to do it successfully!!

Popularity

DR SPOC was a huge hit for all the employees at all levels and very soon, my name became synonymous with DR SPOC!! Some of the new joiners called me DR SPOC without asking my name!! So did some of the managers who came down from the Ireland and UK Offices!! I was ecstatic and was enjoying every moment of the publicity and "feeling of being a mini-celebrity"!!

Fall by jealousy and pride

However, this rosy story had a grim ending as my sycophant manager could not bear to see the publicity and popularity that I had earned in this short span of time. He was even more jealous as the tool developed by my efforts did not have his name on it. He had gone to the extent of entering a heated argument with me with a threatening language to which I bluntly retaliated!! I had even gone to the extent of reporting his atrocities to the senior management and to the HR to shut his mouth!! Subdued, he held this as a grudge and waited for the appropriate moment to unleash his venom!! Spit his venom, he did, which cost me an award and my job!! However, Karma hit back at him as he had to struggle for his promotion and the other team members. He had to even quit his job after a few years in the bid for a promotion!!

Chapter IX – Mortgage Experience

Introduction

Thank you for reading this far to know more about me and my life journey. In this series, I have attempted to capture my professional life journey over the years. In the previous chapter, I described my experience in the telecom company. I wrote about my learning experience, my movement in different departments and my growth path. Due to the rise in favoritism, I had to move out and on, without looking back.

Job in mortgage processing

The next job that I managed to get was in with a mortgage processing company. I had to change cities to get the job, which I gladly accepted. I moved to a new city, a new job, a new life, a new beginning. This new job had plenty in store for me from day one. Lucky me. I was invited to the first anniversary or "birthday" party of the company, which was three days after I joined. I took this opportunity to meet and mingle with different people at different levels. Although, I admit that I am crowd-shy, however, I took this opportunity to overcome some of my shyness.

Communication as a barrier

After the party, it was game on. The additional challenge that I had was of language and communication. Locals preferred their local language for communication. However, I managed to find workarounds to communicate effectively with them in a combination of hybrid and broken languages. In the office, some of my colleagues were amazed to see my knowledge and dedication. I was hired with the sole purpose of setting the foundation of a central support team. Very soon, I realized that I was running short of work thanks to the automation that I managed to do using MS Office products.

Recognition of efforts

Within nine months of joining, I was unanimously promoted to the next level with a salary increment of a whopping 25%!! I was flabbergasted at this!! My hard work and dedication were recognized by a few good men!! This gave my confidence a boost to reach beyond the moon. I continued my performance and very soon, we had a wonderful team setup with multi-dimensional growth. I was thoroughly enjoying my job as it was not monotonous nor was it boring. I was given a multi-faceted challenging role that did not have a fixed job description, rather, I was given subjective responsibilities.

Varied and dynamic role

On a quick recap of my major responsibilities related to my team and department, I was handling financial sub-processes, documents (policy and procedure documents), process and change, internal team audit, the team, technology setup and process, admin support, operations support. My boss had a tough time to figure out my schedule thanks to the variety of tasks that I was handling. The learnings were immense and multi-dimensional. Out of the entire tenure that I spent in this company, I used to spend nearly 26–28 days of the month in office, each workday crossing 12–14 hours consistently.

Synopsis

Although the time spent in office was not much to be proud of, however, I had my reasons for doing so. The prime reason was to fight loneliness. I had my work to do and I "fell in love with my work"!! In the next chapter, I will elaborate on the experiences that I had during my tenure in this company.

Chapter X – Achievements without Designations

Introduction

Thank you for taking the time to read the first nine chapters of my life journey and for supporting me this far. In the previous chapter, I described an overview of my professional journey with a mortgage processing company. The first year of my job saw me through different profiles and responsibilities. I was one of the founding team members of the central support team. My technical expertise was seen and respected by all. They also saw my dedication and loyalty to my job. They saw me working long days and nights single handedly without complaints or fusses, albeit always smiling. However, at that time, I was a very heavy smoker.

Approach to handle tasks

The first year was spent in automation of majority of the small manual routine tasks which helped to save time and free up three resources. One of the managers saw this and collaborated to work with me to setup an automated reporting and email process. We successfully implemented this between two systems as neither of us could be given access to the same paths. So, we resorted to writing macros in excel and outlook to overcome this constraint. I developed a solution-oriented approach to overcome any given situation. The challenging factor was to determine the solution as per the constraints, legal, audit and compliance factors.

Rise to fame

Very soon, other managers started approaching us with their problems with an expectation to get a solution. Our team gained the title of "solution provider" with me leading from the front. I unconsciously resorted to an unconventional thought process considering the constraints from other stakeholders in the same team and department. One of the managers desperately sought our help to hire people for his team. He introduced us to the recruitment team to help in sourcing, identifying and interviewing candidates for the role, for which, my manager and me gladly obliged.

My manager and me had become a force and team to reckon with. Apart from setting processes for our own department, we also did the same thing for other teams and departments. As the team grew, so did our responsibilities and functions. We also setup a centrally accessible support team that handled the primary application across geographies. We would be bombarded with emails from all corners if there would be the smallest issue. Not only would we resolve it within record time, we earned the title of a "go to support team".

Resistance from other colleagues

As our fame spread, so did our enemies. There was one junior and middle management team who did not like our way of functioning, doing work and getting work done. Dirty corporate politics took over the regular functioning of our team operations. It became more and more difficult for us to fight back as this spread faster than venom and wildfire. I had a few personal conversations with my original founding team members and voiced my concerns. They believed me and knew that I was right. They could not dispute me thanks to my reputation that I had managed to build over the months and years. I decided to move out of the company.

Synopsis

When I resigned, there was a loose attempt made to retain me. My peers knew that it was a futile attempt considering the people with whom I had to operate with. Hence, the retention effort was a nominal one for the records. This was what I had learnt about retention efforts and how HR minimizes attrition. Hence, to counter them, I had to think of a valid irrefutable reason. The bigger challenge was to create a perception of circumstances to back my reason. This was a challenge for my immediate supervisors to tackle and their efforts proved futile.

Chapter XI – Remote Assistance Services

Introduction

Thank you for following my life journey and my professional adventures outlined in the first ten chapters of this book. My life journey has been a roller coaster ride of sorts with a variety of learnings at every step. It has been an enduring and testing journey undertaken with sugar and salt all the way. I met a variety of people with different levels of arrogance, tolerance, shrewdness, guile, humility, etc.

Job in a small-scale company

After my last stint with a mortgage processing company, I decided to move out to a smaller sized company that had a different type of business model. I moved to a company that provided virtual assistance services. I was amazed at the level of outsourcing that can happen. The type of jobs that need to be handled are classified, categorized and paid for by people who cannot handle these tasks themselves.

Out here, I learnt about the intricacies of medium to large scale organizations and their hierarchy. Senior management personnel do not like to get bogged down with tasks that are too trivial for their liking or job profile. Hence, they prefer an assistant to tackle these. Thus, they are more dependent on other people for their functioning. They tend to take an approach of a "dictator" – a person who prefers to give guidance for execution, rather than for execution. For this, they are ready to pay huge amounts either in terms of salary or consulting fees (all of these from the company expenses) for another resource to handle these mundane tasks.

Outsourcing as a service

Calendar management, travel arrangements, coordination with other teams and departments, preparing minutes of meetings, approving requests, sending mailers, etc. are some of the tasks that a virtual assistant would handle. My profile was above these in which I had to handle project planning and execution. Luckily, the client that I was working with was very understanding, lenient and cooperative. He was a wonderful leader and mentor. Under his guidance and support, I got plenty of learnings in many aspects. Very importantly, I got the confidence to do something that I had only either heard of or dreamt about doing—share trading.

Learning experience

He helped our team with a course for share trading. We had started the training with a team of eight. Five were eliminated from the course due to lack of interest and non-participation. Of the remaining, I was the only survivor who happened to win his heart and become his favorite. As a result, I got to learn much more than expected from him with a plethora of responsibilities assigned to me. I took the course very seriously and started applying some of the principles in my share trading.

This leader who we were assigned to, strongly believed in self-development and continuous learning. To facilitate this, he would advise and guide us to develop a self-learning calendar with specific goals and tasks. He would also help us track the progress of these. In a way, he used to guide us through a systematic self-learning and self-development process. Sadly, the other members of the team did not believe in this pattern. I did recognize the importance and value of this, hence, I attempted to develop and follow it with a few modifications which worked for me. He too appreciated this approach.

Share trading as a hobby

In August 2016, I opened my share trading account and entered the world of share trading. I realized that it was easier than I thought as I was armed with the basic know how. I developed my strategy based on the core principles that I had learnt. By God's grace, I was able to record a 30% growth in my first year with a whopping 100% positive trades!! My broker has an ongoing "60-day challenge" running in which the participant needs to emerge with a positive balance at the end to be eligible for a brokerage refund during this period. Till date, I have managed to do it consistently 9 times in a row!!

Bonding with client

Coming back to my work life, my client and me had developed a rapport that was beyond professional relations. The bonding that we built with time has grown so strong that it is difficult to break, especially by a third party or an outsider. With him, I learnt about financial statements and their analysis, company structure, company organization, company administration, etc. Very importantly, I learnt about budgeting and forecasting. In other words, I had the foundation laid for becoming an entrepreneur.

Synopsis

Armed with this knowledge, I was able to walk more confidently than before. These changes were very evident especially with the people who worked with me every day. However, I never used to share my knowledge openly with anyone and everyone. The more knowledge and insights I gained, the more I withdrew into my shell. This was the downside of working in a small organization—I realized this the hard way. The next chapter will outline some of the learnings that I have gathered especially a project that I had undertaken and successfully implemented with a hiccup at the end.

Introduction

Thank you for reading the previous eleven chapters of my life journey. By now, you must have seen and got an idea of my experience in various fields over the years. My experience spans different domains at varying levels of roles and responsibilities. It is my rich experience gathered over the years that I pride in!

Recap

In my previous chapter, I mentioned that I got a job in a virtual assistant provider company. The initial project was the development of a small desktop automation tool that was very effective. It involved creating a task management tool in MS Access, which I was able to undertake and complete with finesse. The client was very happy with this and used it extensively to manage his regular personal and professional tasks.

Efficiency improvement project

My major project was an efficiency improvement project that spanned nearly a year. Although the six sigma principles were applied for this project, I nicknamed it the DAVSIM method. DAVSIM stands for **D**ata gathering, **A**nalyze the data, **V**isualize the observations and trends, **S**uggest changes to the process, **I**mplement the process and **M**onitor the process. This is the core methodology for any implementation project, irrespective of size, scale and type.

Approach and methodology

To execute this project, I had to reach out to all the stakeholders repeatedly for continuous inputs. A part of this project also involved research and selection of a tool to help streamline the process. This project had the spice and works—extensive data gathering, primary and derived data sets, analytics and visualizations (using sophisticated tools) supported with storytelling, presentations, extensive research and comparisons using a comparison matrix, selection criteria and procedure, configuration, implementation, training and extensive documentation.

The fun part of this project was the documentation at various stages of the project. That involved gathering requirements, preparing a functional specification document, statement of work, presentation depicting the current scenario, drawbacks, challenges, and suggestions. The visualizations and storytelling were the tricky parts as the data had to be presented in the right way. The implementation part involved memo drafting and circulating to the concerned stakeholders, SOP drafting, approving and circulating, training material preparation, post implementation presentation, training, feedback and monitoring.

I had taken a very systematic approach to this project and had invested plenty of time and effort in understanding every aspect of the project. I had used tools and methods which were alien to me, however, I backed my ability to quickly learn, adapt and adopt something new.

Synopsis

Every good story does have a twist in the tail. This project did go through smoothly. During the transition, there were issues and I had to unexpectedly quit the organization due to a "corporate conspiracy". However, that did not deter me or my intentions to continue my life my way. There was a wealth of knowledge that I had accumulated even during my short stint.

Chapter XIII – Temporary Retirement

Introduction

Thank you for reading the first twelve chapters of my life journey. I have amassed a wealth of learnings and experiences from all the different companies that I was associated with. After the last job, I decided to take a total break from job hunting and working for someone else. I decided to spend some quality time with my family. I managed to spend nearly seven months without active job hunting with my family. By God's Grace, I was able to survive on my savings and help and support from my loving mother and my beloved wife.

Review of my professional career

I took this time to do the below:

- ➢ Reflect upon my entire professional career – gathering what I had learnt over the years.
- ➢ Learnt and implemented share trading with a strategy that I had conceived and developed.
- ➢ Did a couple of odd jobs as a freelancer in a bid to learn something and earn some money.
- ➢ Rejuvenated a few old relationships with some of my old friends, colleagues and acquaintances.
- ➢ Did some research on company formation, nuances, formalities and timelines.
- ➢ Planned my finances and investments to ensure that I do not run high and dry.

All this while, I was at home spending quality time with family. My ex-client in US was in touch with me and very supportive of me during these days. We spent a lot of time in re-building and reconstituting our strategy and approach in the days to come. Although I was not employed, I spent my time getting a feel of early retirement from employment. Yes, it was a fun-filled life with a different feel of the days.

Recap of previous jobs

During my salaried days, I had to follow fixed routines. Some of my previous jobs had highly erratic and irregular job timings. To keep up with these, I had to compromise on my body and family demands to a very large extent. However, this was reversed during my days of retirement.

Although I had retired, I spent a lot of time in rejuvenating myself. This prepared me for the next round of my professional journey. During the latter stages, I started applying for jobs on various online platforms. However, I came across the harsh realization of the toughness and difficulty of getting a job despite being well-experienced.

Last job as a project manager

In March 2017, I did get a job in a startup company as a project manager, however, that was a very short stint for several reasons cited below. Yes, there was a learning curve involved, however, it came at the cost of my self-respect. I saw this early and decided to move out.

- ➢ The management had a dictator style of working and I was not comfortable with that.
- ➢ Salaries were not paid on time.
- ➢ The team consisted of youngsters in their early to mid-twenties, hence, were very aggressive and rebellious.
- ➢ Work environment was very casual and subject to wild mood swings of the management.

However, the only good thing that it did was it gave me temporary support in terms of money. Towards the end of May 2017, I was once again at the crossroads of my life looking at the various options in store for me.

Synopsis

Thank you for reading nearly 95% of my professional journey across various domains, industries, job profiles, roles and responsibilities. I believe that this has helped you to learn quite a bit about professional life and the various nuances of working for someone else. You are constantly watched, judged, molded, pushed, pampered, rubbed the wrong way, encouraged, discouraged, motivated, insulted, et al. Patience, perseverance, persistence and endurance are the keys to facing all these situations and scenarios with a positive mindset and keep moving on.

Chapter XIV – Entrepreneurship

Introduction

Thank you for reaching this far on the concluding chapter of **My Life Journey**. This is just the end of this book, the beginning of another phase of my life journey. I believe that curiosity has brought you this far. Until now, in all the previous chapters, I had described my experiences of how I had applied myself in working for others. In this chapter, I describe how I apply all the gathered experiences in working for myself.

Venture into entrepreneurship

On the 1st of June 2017, I had a discussion with my mother and wife about the way ahead. There were only two options to choose from – either a job or start my own business. Unanimously, both the ladies told me to start my own business. My mother told me that she will give me the initial capital needed to start. My wife assured me that she will be beside me in prayers, morally and emotionally as well. My wife added to the assurance that she will stand beside me, <u>no matter what</u>. This was a huge boost for me as there were no terms and conditions attached to her statement.

The beginning

To begin my journey, I had to evaluate my options and I decided to incorporate my own company. When I saw the list of documents that I had to submit, I realized that I had to speak to my landlord to allow me to use his residential premises for business purposes. He bluntly refused with the reason that he had developed his property purely for residential purposes and not for commercial use. I then went hunting for an office space and came across co-working spaces. This was the beginning and my first baby step. After that, I got my company incorporated by completing all the necessary formalities.

Baby step

I was excited, anxious and happy. The first thing that I made was my own visiting card, albeit crude and my own ID card. In all these years, I had worn a company ID card for someone else; this time, I wore one for my own. It was a different feeling altogether. I was ecstatic. I got my first client. I then started to talk to people who I knew and started soliciting my service offerings based on my skills. It was game on with no turning back, no matter what!

To start, I only had my laptop with a paid version of MS Office installed with a few other free programs that I had downloaded and installed out of curiosity. My first logo was designed using MS Word! I used the various MS Office applications to fulfil my requirements. I still do them till date. In fact, I use MS PowerPoint as a design tool to make logos, flyers, banners, posters signboards, etc. I prefer to be unconventional in my approach and practice it everyday.

Roller coaster ride

Yes, there were times when I had difficulty in getting clients. However, I had developed a habit of learning on the way. I learnt more and more about my own service offering from different people that I had come across. As time went by, I learnt more and more about various aspects of entrepreneurship, for which I have penned a separate book title "Journey of an Entrepreneur".

I was now being approached by more and more people to collaborate and work with. Some people approached me to be their business partner. Very soon, thanks to my activity on social media, I gained popularity. I realized that the best form of marketing is networking with a personalized touch. This forced me to come out of my comfort zone once again. There was a mutation from a shy me to an avid networker.

Amongst some of the learnings that I have gathered are about being consistent, persistent, endurance and perseverance. These are the core qualities of being an enabling entrepreneur. Success is not in reaping in huge amounts of moolah, rather, it lies in not giving up at any point of time. Efforts may fail, however, do not fail to try. This is an age old saying which is easier said than done.

Companies founded

The first company that I had founded in June 2017 was named "Zanzeria Family Consultants (OPC) Private Limited". OPC signifies One Person Company. In this, I am the only director and shareholder. I had started this as a content writing company with more focus on corporate writing. However, I did undertake projects with other type of writing tasks such as case studies, blog writing, web content writing, etc. I learnt more about the business and today, I have a much broader range of service offerings.

The next company that I had incorporated was "Wisewords Interactive Studio Private Limited". This too was a content writing company consisting of two directors and shareholders including me. I had to part ways from this company due to the differences in opinions with the other director.

The next one was "TrillKom InfoWorks Private Limited". This was a community engagement and publication company consisting of two directors and two shareholders I was a director and shareholder, of the other two members, one was only a director and the third was only a shareholder. This was my first venture into publication and media. Unfortunately, I had to part ways due to stark differences in working styles and differences in opinions with the other stakeholders of the company.

I had also been invited to be a part of a trust named "TrillKom Foundation" which is a "media convergence sanctuary". Although there has not been much progress on this front with the other trustee, I have parted ways with this trust purely because I was not able to devote quality time to do justice to my role as a "Deputy Managing Trustee".

The last and recent company incorporated by me is "Inmutatio Consulere Private Limited". This is different from the others primarily because of the nomenclature and the theme. The names are latin words which mean "process of change consultants". This company has two directors and shareholders.

A list of companies and their related service offerings is mentioned in the "About the Author" section of this book. Thanks to the number of companies incorporated and managed, I have had a number of interactions with company secretaries, chartered accountants and other professionals and entrepreneurs in various fields. Hence, I am well versed with the various aspects of company incorporation, especially of a private limited company, the documentation to be completed and the compliances to be adhered to.

Synopsis

I started attending various networking events to build my network of personal and business contacts. Yes, there were the challenges, however, it was fun, and I enjoy it till today. Entrepreneurship is a lifestyle and is about enjoying the roller coaster ride. During my journey, I met many people of different thought processes. I came across different entrepreneurship communities – some paid and some free. I continue to enjoy my onward journey as an enabling entrepreneur...

Thank you for reading about **My Life Journey**. I hope that you have found it a good read and worth the time and learnings. I have simply shared my personal life experiences that I have lived and cherished. My contact info is given in the Appendix. Do feel free to reach out to me if you want to write a similar story about your life journey or any other book and I will be happy to do it for you.

About the Author

Ayaz is an out of the box thinker and loves to look beyond the obvious. He has the uncanny knack of spotting things where people generally overlook or oversee. He is an avid fan of continuous learning and firmly believes that every interaction is a learning experience. Hence, he seeks to learn something new from everyone every day.

During his professional career, he has consistently delivered award-winning performances as an eminent team-player. Often, he has been an unsung hero – delivering performances without hogging the limelight. He has come across many managers with different managing styles and approaches, the good, the bad and the ugly. He has chosen to extract, learn and implement the good from each.

He believes that entrepreneurship is a thought process and a lifestyle that can be adopted by anyone and applied to personal and professional life. He had his stints of entrepreneurship from the early stages of his life. He had learnt a bit about business the old-fashioned way from his father. He had learnt how to manage a distributed setup and different people in different locations.

Amongst one of his earlier ventures was that of an internet café or a cybercafé, which did not give him the returns as he had envisaged. Nevertheless, he had not let his failure bog him down. Rather, he simply moved on to get a job and advance his career. He took all his jobs as learning various aspects of the business, the different sub-entities within the larger umbrella and how they gel together.

Armed with that knowledge and experience, he is currently heading two ventures:

1. **ZANZERIA FAMILY CONSULTANTS (OPC) Pvt Ltd.**
   a. Written and Media Content Development.
   b. Specializing in short text/musical videos.
   c. Tutorial Video Series.
   d. Visual representations – static or graphical.
   e. Personal Finance Management.
   f. Mentoring and Consulting.

Tag Line: **a written and media content development studio**

Associated Brand(s):

> **Artismatic Magnifico** – artistic creativity in its charismatic magnificence.

2. **INMUTATIO CONSULERE Pvt Ltd.**
   a. Business Process Improvement.
   b. Voice of Customer Analysis.
   c. Customer Experience Enhancement Program.
   d. Business Publications.
   e. Leadership and Organizational Development.
   f. Corporate Branding and Communication.

Tag Line: **re-imagine » re-think » re-engineer**

Associated Brand(s):

> **Azimuth** – Customer Driven Initiatives to Improve Business Processes
> **Chrysalis** – Enhancing Leadership Skills for Effective Change Management
> **Lexicon** – Redefining Corporate Communications

A bit about his history, he was born and brought up in the Island city of Mumbai where he spent nearly 35 years of his life. He has worked in several companies in different roles and fulfilled different responsibilities as required by the businesses.

The primary strength that Ayaz has is the ability to learn quickly. He has not done too many courses apart from completing his Bachelor's in Automobile Engineering. All his skills have been acquired and polished practically on the job.

Ayaz is straightforward and blunt, which is resented by many. He firmly believes that an initial ugly bluntness is far better than hidden rosy falseness. It is this approach coupled with a never give up attitude and approach that has kept him going through various hardships of life.

He has been approached by many for various reasons. For consulting, mentoring, counselling, advice, business partnerships, business projects, to name a few. He was involved in founding and setting up a few companies from which he has moved out for various reasons (personal and professional).

Although not very good at marketing or selling, he has an uncanny knack of striking good conversations even with little knowledge of the topic. He believes that learning is a never-ending process that never stops at any age or designation. Another reason for being open to learning is his belief in change is constant. Change is inevitable and will happen. Hence, rather than resist change, welcome it with open arms.

Ayaz does not believe in money making gimmicks or get rich quick schemes. Rather he prefers to take the slow and steady consistent and sustainable approach for making money. He has tried this approach with his knowledge of share trading which is paying him rich dividends.

Appendix

The simplest way is to type "Ayaz Zanzeria" in google search. The search results will give a listing of all his websites, social media profiles and other listings on other websites. Specific contact info is as below.

Company Websites

- ❖ https://thezanzeriafamily.com
- ❖ https://artismatic.gallery
- ❖ https://inmutatio.com

Personal Websites

- ❖ https://ayazzanzeria.page
- ❖ https://thejanz.rocks

Professional Contact

- ❖ ayaz@thezanzeriafamily.com
- ❖ ayaz@inmutatio.com
- ❖ Call/Text/WhatsApp: +91 80955 03465 / +91 63606 17899
- ❖ Skype: ayaz.zanzeria / ayaz@thezanzeriafamily.com

Personal Contact

- ❖ hi@ayazzanzeria.page
- ❖ ayaz@thejanz.rocks
- ❖ ayaz.zanzeria@hotmail.com
- ❖ ayazzanzeria@gmail.com

www.ingramcontent.com/pod-product-compliance
Lightning Source LLC
Chambersburg PA
CBHW070519220526
45467CB00002B/752